Neptune's Underwater Empire

Children's Greek & Roman Myths

BABY PROFESSOR

EDUCATION KIDS

Speedy Publishing LLC
40 E. Main St. #1156
Newark, DE 19711
www.speedypublishing.com

In this book, you will enter the underwater world of the Roman god Neptune. Read on and learn about the god of fresh water and the sea.

Who is Neptune?

He was the lord of the sea in Roman mythology. The Romans also worshiped him as the god of horses, for it was believed that Neptune was the creator of horses. He was given the name Neptune Equester as the patron of horse-racing.

Let us learn interesting facts about him.

He was the brother
of Jupiter, the king
of all the gods, and
Pluto, the king of
the underworld.
When their father
Saturn died, they
divided the world
among themselves.
Jupiter took the
heavens, Pluto took
the underworld
and Neptune
took the sea.

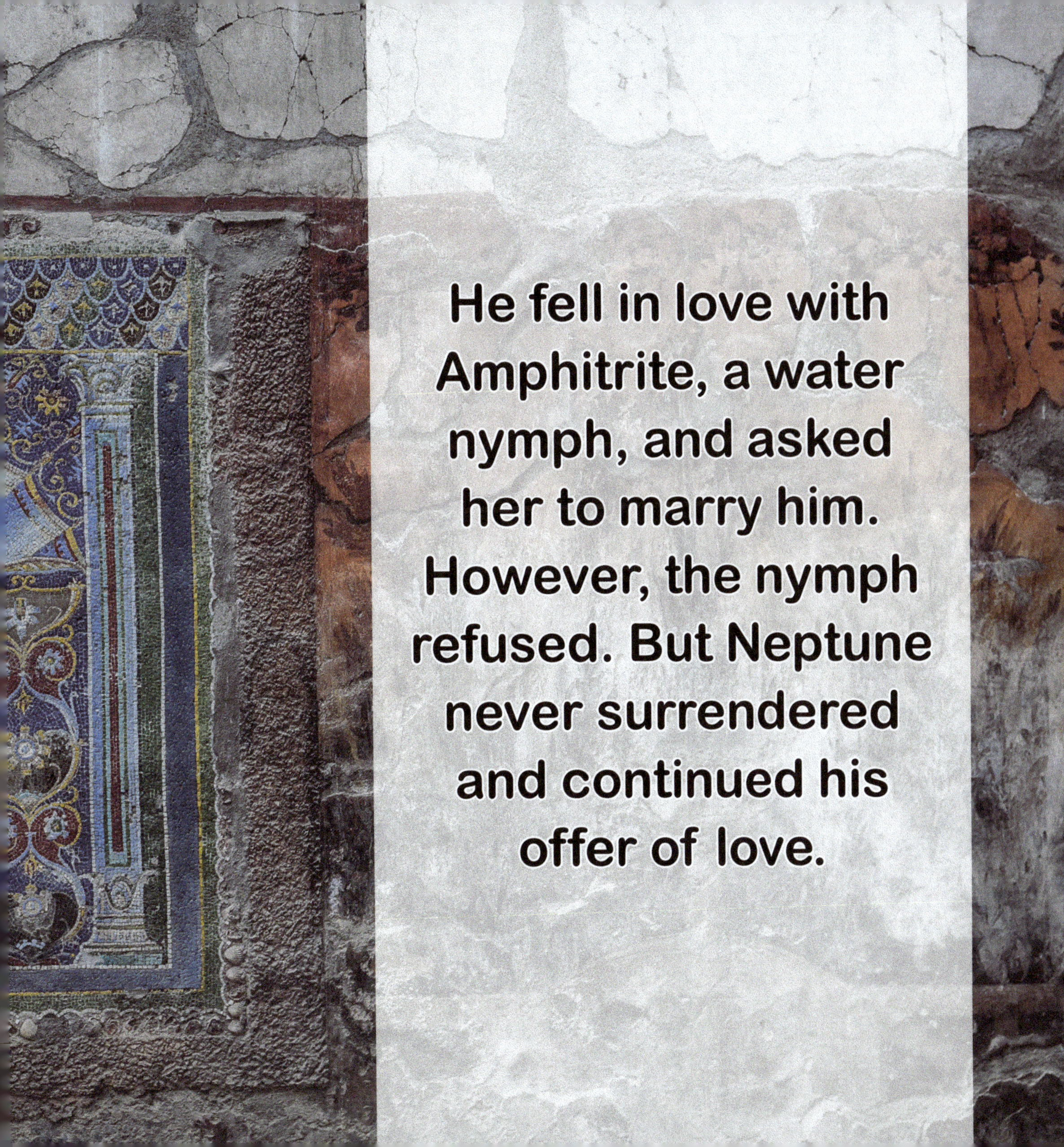

He fell in love with
Amphitrite, a water
nymph, and asked
her to marry him.
However, the nymph
refused. But Neptune
never surrendered
and continued his
offer of love.

He sent a dolphin
to watch over
Amphitrite and
to persuade her,
and she finally
changed her mind.
Neptune and
Amphitrite had
several children.

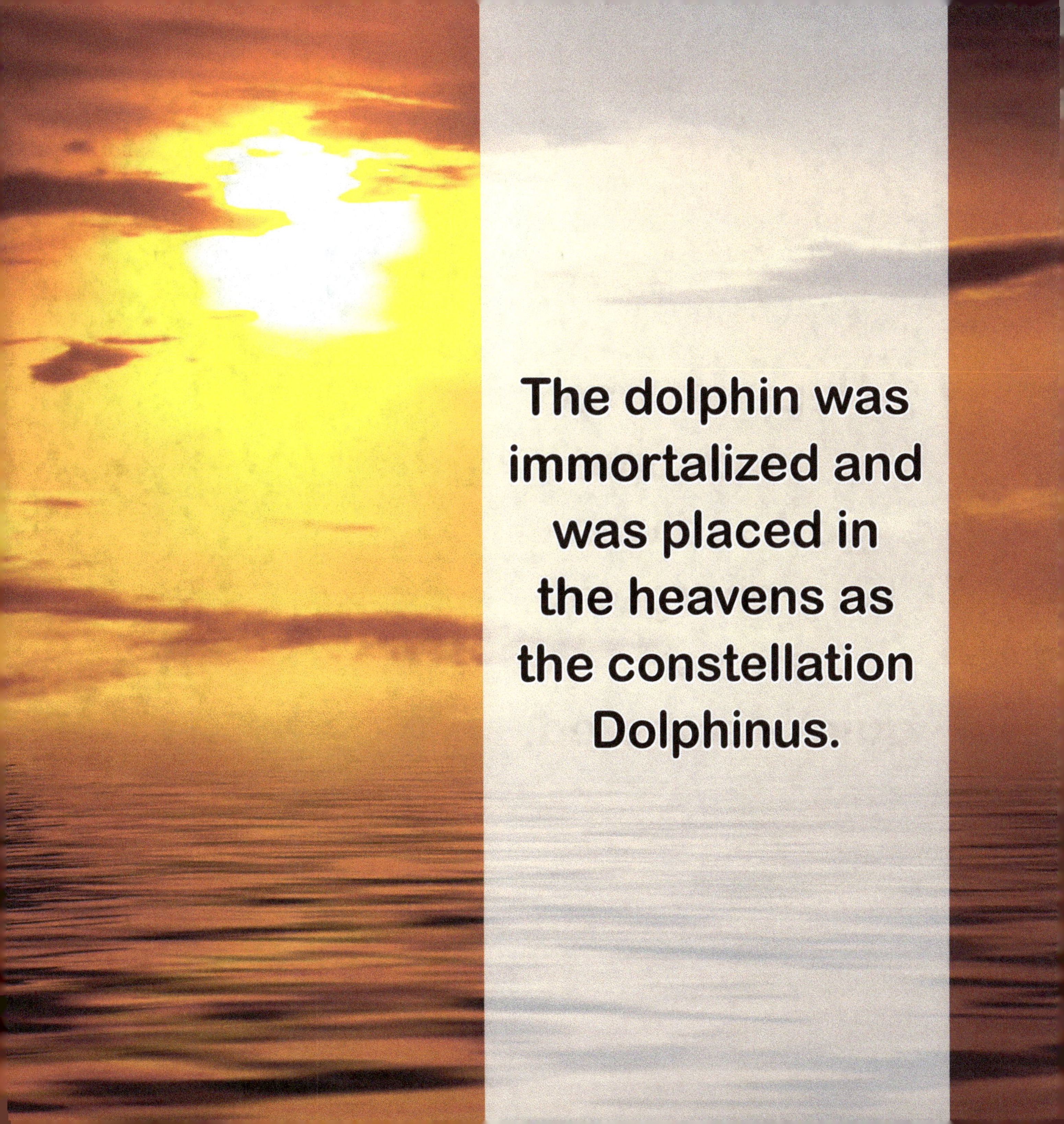
The dolphin was immortalized and was placed in the heavens as the constellation Dolphinus.

Neptune was
a handsome
god and was
very energetic.
He was
quick-tempered.

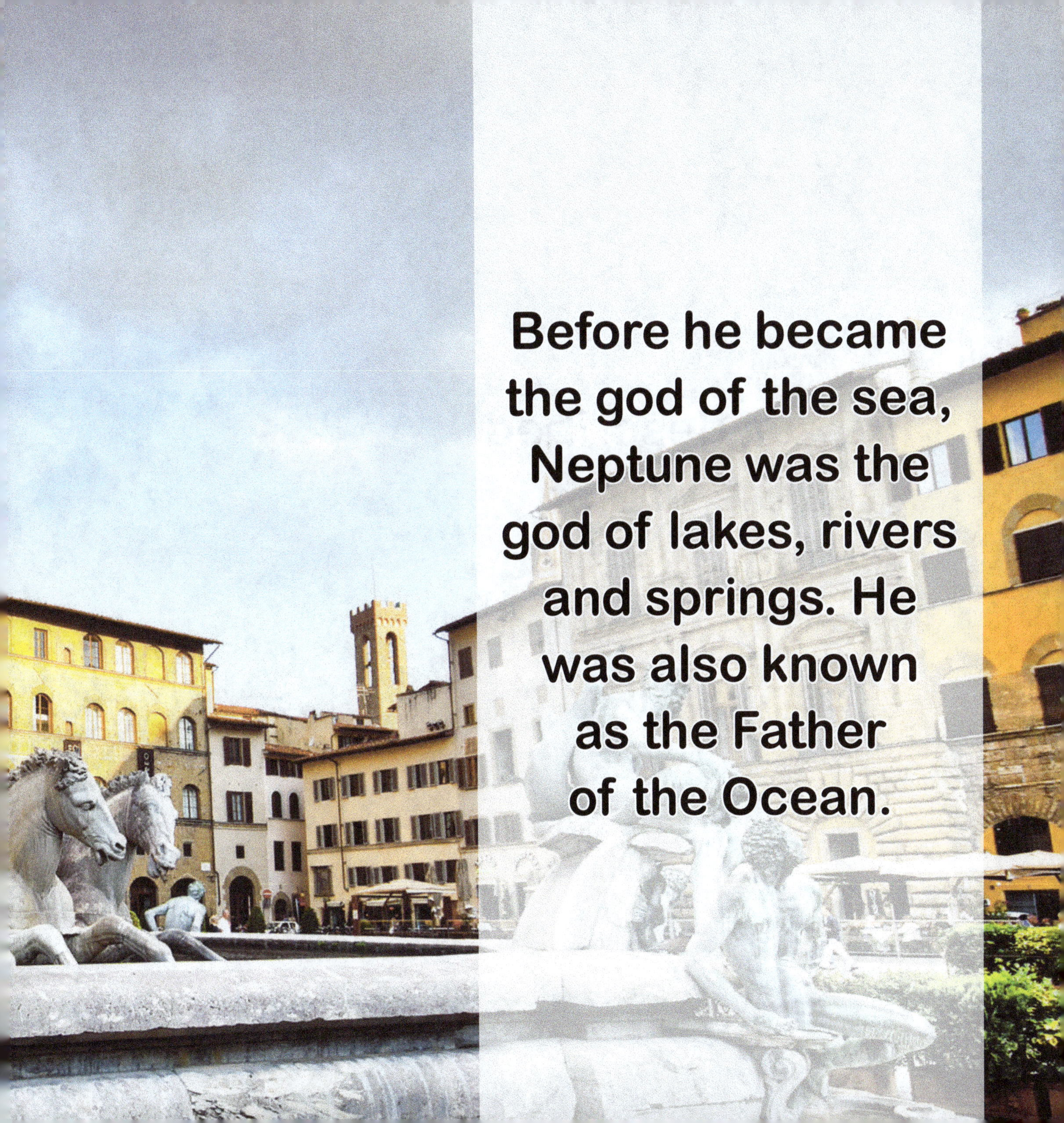

Before he became
the god of the sea,
Neptune was the
god of lakes, rivers
and springs. He
was also known
as the Father
of the Ocean.

He was described as the god of earthquakes and was known as the "Earthshaker".

Neptune's Greek counterpart was the ancient god of the sea, Poseidon.

He was the son of
Saturn and Opis,
the earth mother.

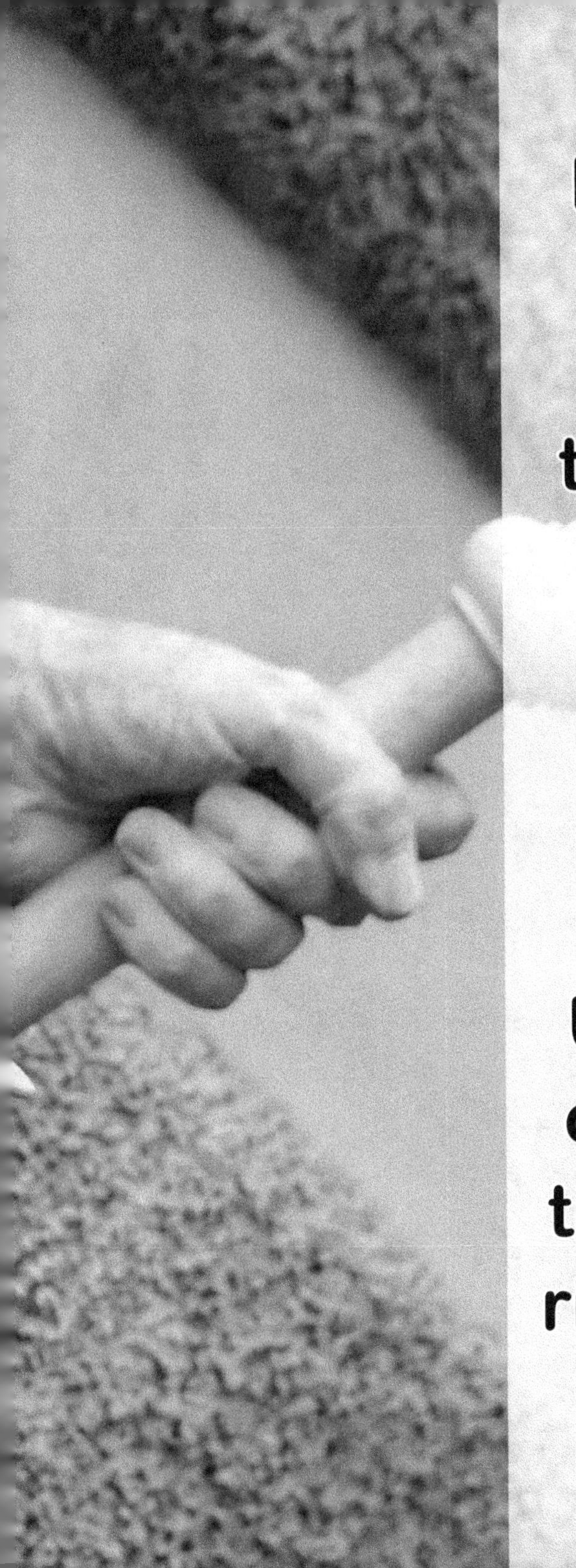

His symbols include the horse and the trident, which is a three-pronged spear used for catching fish. Neptune's trident and would allow him to control bodies of water. Using the trident, he could cause horrible tidal waves and could rise water pressure to cause earthquakes.

The planet
Neptune was
named by
scientists after
him because its
deep blue gas
clouds resembled
the great oceans
and seas of Earth.

A temple was
built for him in
Rome near Circus
Flaminius, which
was a great
racetrack.

He is one of the
Olympians with
godly strength and
power. His being
immortal made
him immune to
earthly diseases.
He was one of
the strongest
Olympian gods.

Neptune was
amphibious. He
could survive in
water and air.
He could swim
at superhuman
speed. He had
the power to
communicate with
all sea creatures.
Neptune
was often
characterized
as ill-tempered
and violent.

There is more to
know Neptune.
Research more
and have fun!

Visit
BABY PROFESSOR
EDUCATION KIDS
www.BabyProfessorBooks.com
to download Free Baby Professor eBooks and view
our catalog of new and exciting Children's Books